Discover
ANCIENT
SUMER

Paul Collins

Illustrations by
Niall Stewart Harding

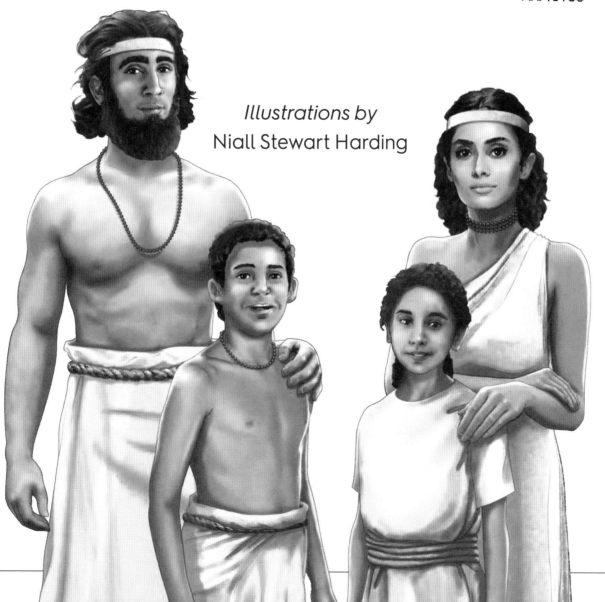

Discover the world of ancient Sumer ...

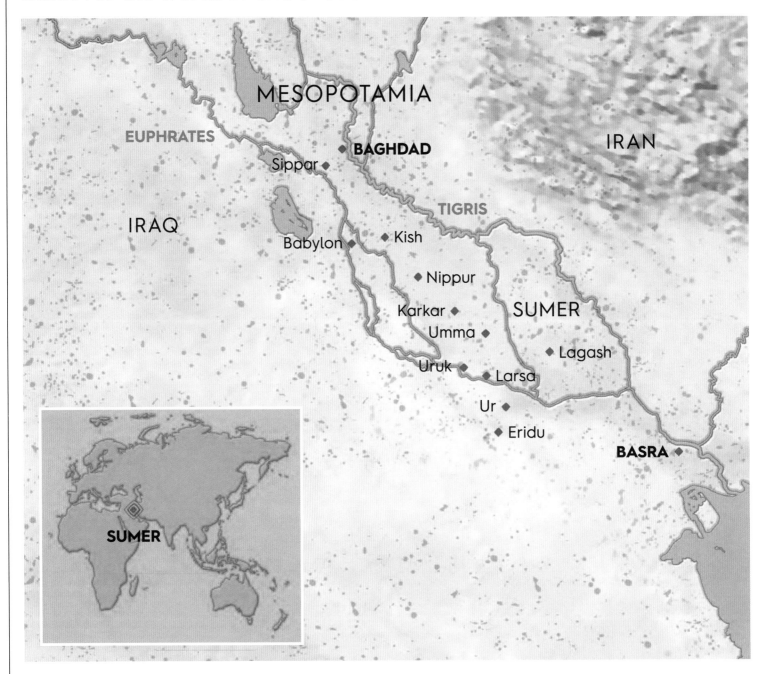

MESOPOTAMIA

EUPHRATES

IRAN

Sippar ◆ **BAGHDAD**

IRAQ

TIGRIS

Babylon ◆ ◆ Kish

◆ Nippur

Karkar ◆ SUMER

Umma ◆

◆ Lagash

Uruk ◆ ◆ Larsa

Ur ◆

◆ Eridu

BASRA ◆

SUMER

▶ **Urlam** and **Namma** are brother and sister. They live in Sumer and will help you to discover their home.

Contents

Where and when?

This book is about a region of the ancient world that we call Sumer. Today this is the southern part of Iraq. It is a vast, flat land of floodplains formed by the Rivers Tigris and Euphrates. It was here that some of the world's first cities arose and writing was invented.

Did you know?

The ancient Greeks called the area 'Mesopotamia', which means 'between the rivers'.

The climate is very hot in summer, but it is cooler for a few months in winter. There is little rain and dust storms can be common.

Each year, between April and June, the rivers would flood. The soil carried in the floodwaters helped to make the land fertile. But from time to time the floods would be much heavier and even destructive. The rivers might change their course, cutting new channels across the floodplains and washing away farmland and settlements.

The first people to settle in Sumer, around 6000 BC, lived in small villages close to the rivers. They hunted animals, farmed the land, herded sheep, pigs, goats and cattle and fished the rivers.

Buildings were made from mud bricks or reeds, gathered from the marshes that covered large areas of Sumer. Some people living in the marshes still use the ancient methods of building today to make very impressive houses.

Reeds were also used to make mats, baskets and even boats. These could be made watertight with a covering of bitumen, a black, sticky substance formed from crude oil. It can be scooped from naturally occurring nearby pools.

NEXT **Discover** how we know about the people of ancient Sumer

Excavating Sumer

Archaeologists have explored the remains of some of Sumer's ancient settlements. They have made remarkable discoveries at places such as Uruk, Ur, Eridu, Nippur, Kish and Lagash. These show that the people of Sumer, who we call the Sumerians, were great artists, builders, inventors, warriors and traders.

The first excavations by British, French and American archaeologists took place over 150 years ago. Many of the objects uncovered in these excavations can be found in museums around the world. In 1926, however, a museum was opened in Baghdad, the capital of Iraq. Today everything discovered by archaeologists stays in the country.

▲ The Iraq Museum in Baghdad

It is sometimes possible to find an ancient site on the flat plains of southern Iraq because it will form a mound. This is described by archaeologists as a *tell* (from the Arabic word for 'hill' or 'mound'). Tells were created by people rebuilding their mud buildings and throwing away their rubbish on the same site for hundreds or even thousands of years. The most recent levels of the tell will therefore be found at the top and the oldest levels at the very bottom.

Iraqi and foreign archaeologists continue to explore the tells of ancient Sumer to learn more about the Sumerians.

Did you know?

There are at least 10,000 archaeological sites across Iraq and only a few have been excavated.

NEXT
Discover how the Sumerians farmed the land and what they ate and drank

Farming and food

Because there was little rainfall for most of the year, farmers took water from the rivers to grow their crops. It was easy to dig a ditch to bring water to fields and orchards near a river, but larger irrigation canals were needed to reach land further away. As some villages grew into towns, the digging of canals became important. The canals were needed to make the land more fertile so it could produce enough food for all the people.

Did you know?

The most important crop was barley. The grains were ground into flour to make bread. Barley was also used to make a low-alcohol beer. The Sumerians drank this using straws to avoid swallowing bits of the barley.

▶ Cylinder seal impression showing people drinking beer through straws

Dates were another very important food. They could be eaten fresh, stored for long periods, or turned into a syrup to sweeten other foods. Vegetables included lettuces and cucumbers.

The main farm animals in Sumer were cattle, goats and sheep. Butter and cheese could be made from milk. Wool was plucked from sheep rather than cut with shears, and cattle hides were made into leather. The wool and leather were then used to make clothes.

The Sumerians caught fish in the rivers and collected shellfish from the sea. Fishermen used nets and fish hooks at the end of lines. Wild animals such as gazelle and boar were hunted for their meat with bows and arrows.

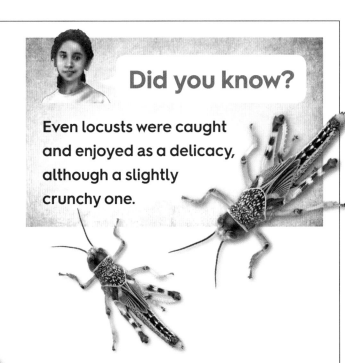

Did you know?

Even locusts were caught and enjoyed as a delicacy, although a slightly crunchy one.

◄ A fish hook excavated near Kish

NEXT

Discover about the world's first cities

Cities of Sumer

By 3500 BC the populations of some towns had grown into cities. The largest was certainly Uruk, which had a population of at least 10,000 people. At this time no other settlement on the planet was as big as Uruk.

Did you know?

Thousands of bricks would have been made quickly using moulds and then left to harden in the hot sun.

At the centre of Uruk stood huge, mud brick buildings. They may have been temples or perhaps gathering places for important Sumerians to do business. The walls of the buildings were covered in plaster. Sections of the walls were decorated with thousands of small clay cones, their sharp ends pushed into the walls and the blunt ends, dipped in different coloured paints, arranged to form mosaics. This form of decoration was used on similar large buildings throughout Mesopotamia.

At a later date Uruk was surrounded by a massive mud brick wall with gates.

▲ **Clay cone mosaic decoration from Uruk**

Work in Sumer

Hundreds of people farmed the surrounding land to supply enough food for the population of the city. Workers in the fields cut the barley, using sickles made of clay. These were made in moulds and then baked in ovens to make them hard. When a sickle broke, it was very cheap to replace it.

▼ Clay sickle (and modern version)

Other people had the job of making pottery vessels on a wheel. The pots were baked in ovens to harden the clay so that they could hold liquids such as water, milk and vegetable oils, as well as dry foods. One of the most common bowls was made by hand, perhaps with a mould. These may have been used to bake loaves of bread of roughly the same size.

The city leaders had to find ways to manage and feed all these workers, whether they were farmers, builders or potters. To help them do this they invented writing.

Did you know?

Just like pots, reed baskets were used as containers but they don't survive for archaeologists to find.

▲ Hand-made bowls for bread

▶ Making a clay beer pot

Discover how writing was invented

Writing

Writing was invented by the Sumerians around 3200 BC. It is one of the most important inventions in the history of humankind. Through their writings we can learn about the Sumerians from their own words.

The first kind of writing was picture writing. To record barley, for example, a picture of a stem of barley was drawn to create a 'pictogram'. The Sumerians used a sharpened piece of reed on a small tablet of soft, damp clay, which they held in the palm of one hand. Small circles beside the pictogram are numbers. The most widely used system involved counting in units of 10 and 60.

In this way the Sumerians could record the amount of food put into storerooms, the size of fields and who owned them. They could also note the numbers of farm animals, slaves and other workers. The tablets were also used to record payment of different amounts of grain, beer and vegetable oils to people, depending on how important they were.

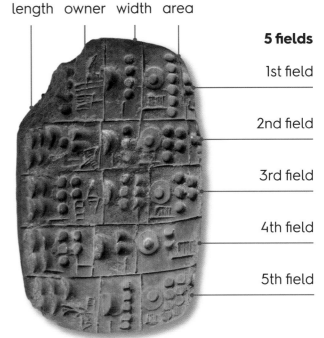

Field

length   owner   width   area

5 fields

1st field

2nd field

3rd field

4th field

5th field

▲ **Early tablet 3000 BC (actual size)**

▶ **Writing cuneiform on a clay tablet**

The people responsible for writing tablets, known as scribes, needed to learn hundreds of signs. Over time the scribes started to combine pictograms in order to write words in the Sumerian language. Sumerian was not the only language spoken in Sumer, but it must have been the most important one. Other people spoke a language we call Akkadian, similar to modern Arabic.

Early tablets were divided into a grid to record information. Each cell was filled with pictograms and numbers, like a modern spreadsheet.

Later, the signs were arranged in rows and read from left to right. The signs also became less like pictures; instead scribes pressed the sharpened reed into the clay to leave combinations of little, nail-like wedges. We call this type of writing 'cuneiform', from the Latin word 'cuneus' meaning 'wedge'.

Sin-ka-shi-id
Sin-kashid

Nita kal-ga
mighty man

Lugal unu-ka
king of Uruk

Lugal-am-na-nu-um
king of the Amnanum tribe

u-a
provider

e-an-na
of the Eanna Temple

▲ **Later tablet 2000 BC (actual size)**

Did you know?

Pictographic signs became cuneiform or 'wedge-like' after many hundreds of years.

Original pictogram	Later cuneiform	Original meaning
		bird
		fish
		donkey
		ox
		sun, day
		grain
		orchard

NEXT

Discover how the Sumerians protected their belongings

Seals and sealing

The people responsible for the storerooms of temples and palaces needed to keep their contents safe and secure. To help them, they used seals.

The earliest seals were small pieces of stone carved with a design. The seal often had a hole drilled through it so that it could be hung from a piece of string. Some seals were worn as a necklace or tied to a belt.

The seal's design was stamped into a small lump of clay covering the knot of a rope tying shut a basket, box, bag or even a door. Only the seal owner or the correct official would have been allowed to break the seal impression to gain access.

From around 3500 BC, people in Sumer started to use a new type of seal. Known as a cylinder seal, it was made from a small cylinder of stone, drilled through its length and carved with a design. The cylinder seal could be rolled over damp clay to leave an impression.

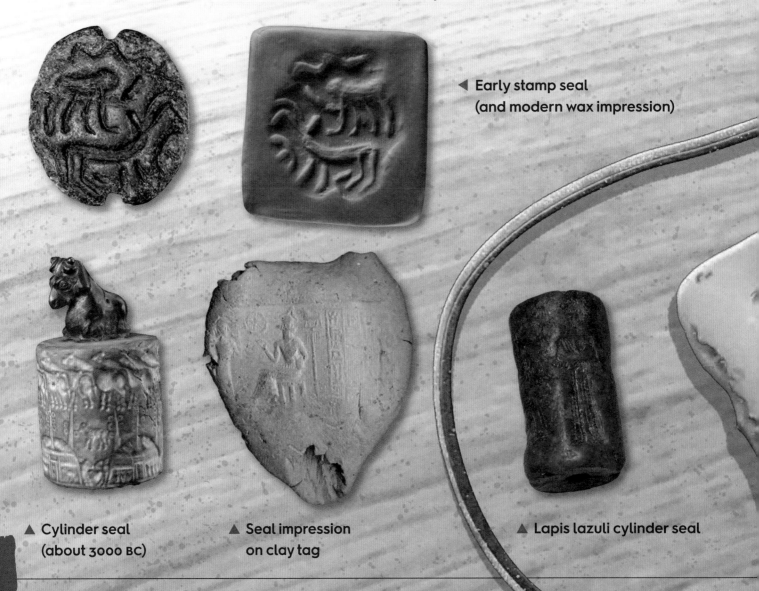

◄ Early stamp seal
(and modern wax impression)

▲ Cylinder seal
(about 3000 BC)

▲ Seal impression
on clay tag

▲ Lapis lazuli cylinder seal

A cylinder seal had space to carve more images than was possible on a stamp seal. As a result, seal-makers could show scenes of everyday life as well as gods and monsters. They also added cuneiform inscriptions.

Seals were often made of limestone, a type of grey-white stone found in Sumer, or of shell from the sea. The most precious and expensive stone used by the Sumerians was lapis lazuli – a beautiful blue stone found only in the region of Afghanistan, many thousands of kilometres to the east of Sumer. This stone was carried to Sumer overland or by sea.

▶ **Rolling a cylinder seal on clay**

Did you know?

The Sumerians believed that lapis lazuli had magical properties and associated the stone with kings, gods and heroes.

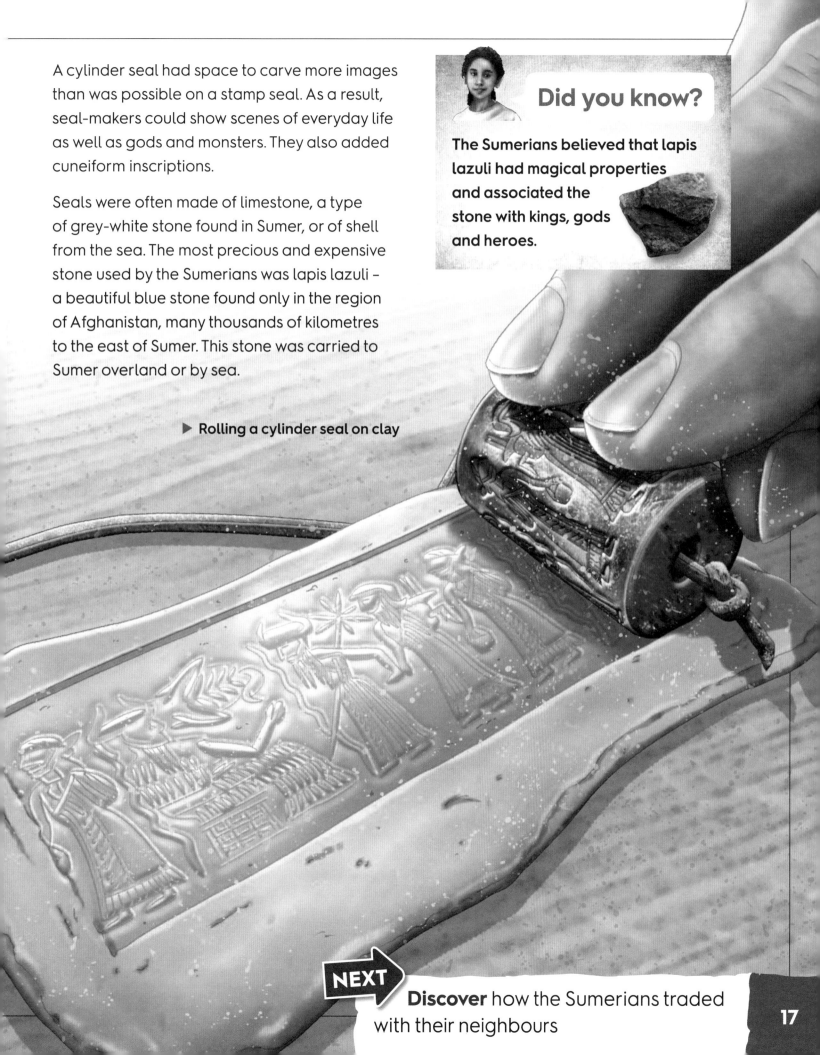

NEXT

Discover how the Sumerians traded with their neighbours

Transport and trade

The villages, towns and cities of Sumer were connected by rivers and canals. Different types of boats, made from reeds or wood, were used to transport people, animals, agricultural products and objects. Some cities had docks where the goods could be loaded and unloaded.

On land goods would be carried by hand, or on the backs of people or donkeys.

A sledge, pulled by donkeys or oxen, was used to thresh (crush) stems of barley to separate the grains for grinding. By around 3200 BC the Sumerians had fitted solid wheels to some sledges to create carts. This meant that roads also became important for connecting settlements. It was, however, more expensive to move goods by road rather than by boat.

Cloth was woven not only from the wool of sheep, but also from fibres of the flax plant to make linen. Many of these textiles were used by people in Sumer, but they were also one of the region's most important exports. The cloth would have been transported by boat or on the backs of donkeys to places outside Sumer where it could be exchanged for other goods.

Some of the most prized and expensive materials came to Sumer from the mountainous lands to the east and north. They included timber for building, metals (especially copper and tin, melted together to make bronze, as well as gold and silver), and stones such as blue lapis lazuli from Afghanistan and red carnelian from India.

Did you know?

These precious and expensive materials were especially important for kings, as they could show how wealthy and powerful these rulers were.

▲ Lapis and carnelian necklace

NEXT **Discover** Sumerian kings, queens and commoners

Kings, queens and commoners

The most important people in Sumer were the rulers of small kingdoms. Each kingdom had a capital city with towns and villages in the surrounding farmland. The different kingdoms and their cities were connected by the region's rivers and canals.

▶ Sumerian votive figure, perhaps of a king

The king lived in a palace with his queen and their family. Palaces were large mud brick buildings with a number of rooms:

- **A THRONE ROOM**
  where people could be presented to the king

- **COURTYARDS**
  where gifts and supplies could be unloaded

- **BEDROOMS**

- **BATHROOMS**

- **KITCHEN**

- **STOREROOMS**

- **WORKSHOPS**
  where palace staff produced textiles, metal and stone objects

- **OFFICES**
  for the scribes; here they kept letters, receipts and accounts, among other cuneiform tablets

The king and queen had their own personal servants and each owned their own farmland, on which they employed many workers. When the king died one of his sons (usually, but not always, the eldest) became ruler in his place.

Ordinary people lived in small houses made from mud bricks. Houses had wooden doors and very small windows. These helped to protect the house from the heat of the sun and dust storms, and also prevented wild animals from entering. Inside the house tiny rooms were arranged around a central courtyard, open to the sky.

It was here that cooking, weaving and pottery making took place. The courtyard was a cool, shaded space during the day and a warm, safe place at night.

Did you know?

Furniture, such as chairs and tables, was for the rich; most people sat on mats and cushions.

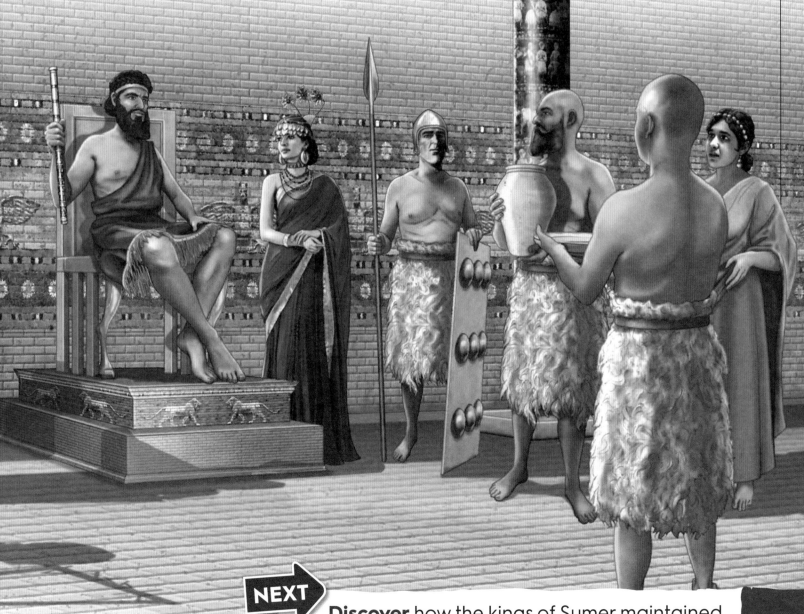

NEXT

Discover how the kings of Sumer maintained peace, but sometimes went to war

War and peace

One of the most important jobs of the ruler of each kingdom was to ensure that peace and order existed in their territory. Lists of laws were written down so that the kings could show they took justice for their people very seriously.

Agreements, or treaties, were made between the different kingdoms of Sumer so that trade, farming and fishing could also take place peacefully. Through these written records we know which kingdom controlled which rivers, canals, roads and farmland. If another kingdom wanted to use any of these, they had to make a payment.

However, sometimes there were disagreements between neighbouring kingdoms about who owned what. This could lead to disputes or even war.

A war between the kingdoms of Umma and Lagash lasted on and off for over 100 years. We know about the war because the rulers of Lagash set up monuments recording their victories – but from these we only have their side of the story. Fighting is said to have been about some farmland belonging to Lagash that the people of Umma had been using without paying rent.

Some kings used their armies to conquer other kingdoms, or to undertake raids into the mountains to the east of Sumer. Here they could plunder towns for stones, metals and slaves. Chariots pulled by donkeys were used by soldiers carrying spears, while other soldiers marched on foot. Along with spears, the main weapons were bows and arrows and axes. Captured people were put to work, but enemy soldiers might be executed.

Around 2300 BC King Sargon, ruler of the city of Agade, conquered all the Sumerian cities and created an empire. After this the people came to believe that only one city could ever rule over the whole of Sumer. The Sumerian King List was written to suggest that this had always been true. It claimed that it was the gods who decided which city should dominate Sumer – and also when that city should be replaced by another.

▲ Sumerian King List

NEXT

Discover some of the gods of Sumer

Religion

The Sumerians believed that humans had been created by the gods as their servants. Each of the cities in Sumer was thought to be the home of a powerful god or goddess; all the cities together controlled everything. The gods were known by different names across Sumer, depending on which language the people spoke (see page 15). For example, the Sumerian goddess Inana was known to Akkadian speakers as Ishtar.

INANA

Sumerian name	Inana
Akkadian name	Ishtar
City	Uruk

Responsibility
A powerful goddess of love and war. The queen of heaven, she appeared in the sky as the planet we call Venus.

ENKI

Sumerian name	Enki
Akkadian name	Ea
City	Eridu

Responsibility
A god who lived in a fresh water ocean (called the Abzu) underneath the earth; he helped make the lands fertile.

NANNA

Sumerian name	Nanna
Akkadian name	Sin
City	Ur

Responsibility
The moon god, often shown as a bull with horns like a crescent.

ENLIL

Sumerian name	Enlil
Akkadian name	Ellil
City	Nippur

Responsibility
One of the most powerful gods: associated with kings, he decided their future.

UTU

Sumerian name	Utu
Akkadian name	Shamash
City	Sippar

Responsibility
God of the sun, his light and warmth allowed plants and crops to grow. He was also associated with justice.

AN

Sumerian name	An
Akkadian name	Anu
City	Uruk

Responsibility
The god of the sky and father of the gods.

ISHKUR

Sumerian name	Ishkur
Akkadian name	Adad
City	Karkar

Responsibility
The god of storms which brought fertile rain but could cause damage, so he was also associated with war.

NEXT

Discover where the gods lived, and how they were fed and clothed

Temples and ziggurats

The gods of Sumer were believed to need many of the same things as ordinary humans: clothes, food, drink and a house to live in. Their 'houses' were the temples built by their human servants.

Temples were often built on mudbrick platforms, so they had to be approached by steps or a ramp. Raising the building above the level of ordinary houses made them appear special and important – so suitable dwelling places for the gods.

Although larger than ordinary homes, temples were not especially big: most people would have had to gather in the courtyard outside. Only priests may have entered the temple itself. Inside the building they offered food and drink to a statue of the god, which was also provided with clothes and jewellery.

Some rich men and women had small stone statues made to represent themselves, and these were given to the gods. The figures stand with their hands held together, perhaps as a mark of respect or in prayer.

Did you know?

Sometimes men and women are shown wearing fleece skirts or dresses. Sheep were often sacrificed to the gods in Sumer, so a woollen fleece may have been a special religious outfit.

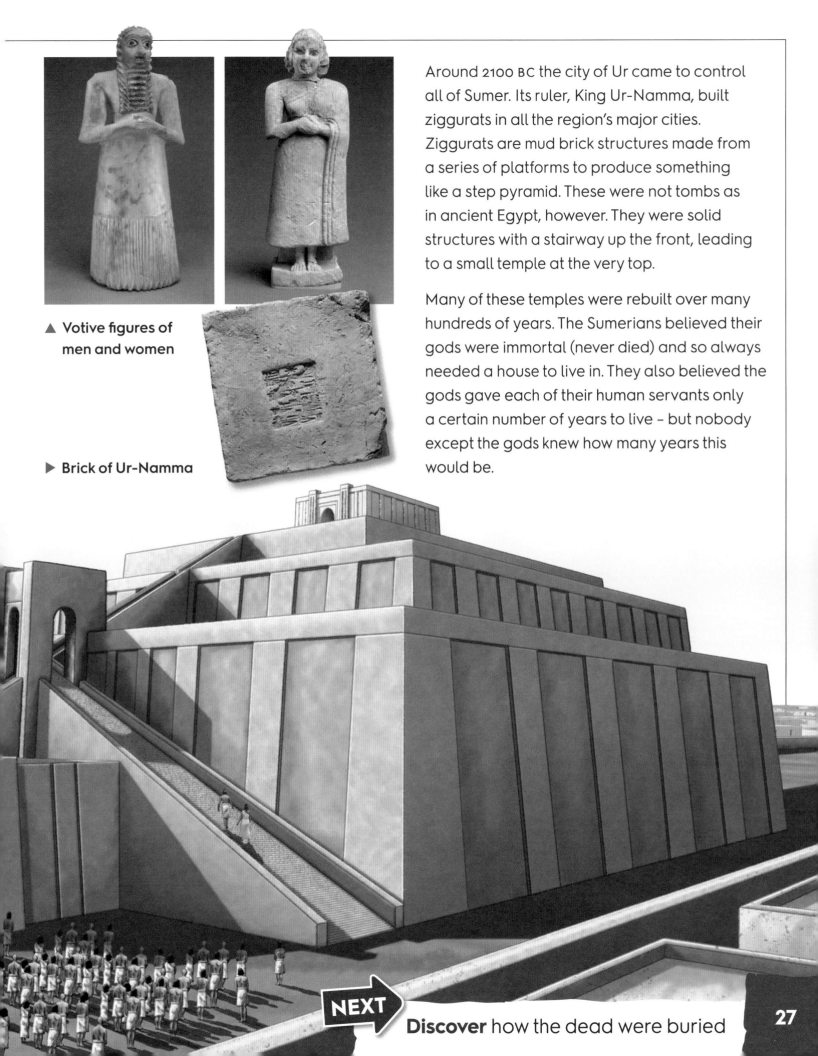

▲ Votive figures of men and women

▶ Brick of Ur-Namma

Around 2100 BC the city of Ur came to control all of Sumer. Its ruler, King Ur-Namma, built ziggurats in all the region's major cities. Ziggurats are mud brick structures made from a series of platforms to produce something like a step pyramid. These were not tombs as in ancient Egypt, however. They were solid structures with a stairway up the front, leading to a small temple at the very top.

Many of these temples were rebuilt over many hundreds of years. The Sumerians believed their gods were immortal (never died) and so always needed a house to live in. They also believed the gods gave each of their human servants only a certain number of years to live – but nobody except the gods knew how many years this would be.

NEXT

Discover how the dead were buried

Death and burial

The Sumerians carefully wrapped dead bodies in cloth or placed them in a reed coffin for burial in a grave. Each body was buried with a few of the person's belongings. Some people were buried beneath a room in their family home, while others were buried in large cemeteries.

In the centre of Ur was a very large cemetery, with one area set aside for the graves of kings and queens. Each royal grave was a big pit, several metres deep, with a slope leading down to the bottom. On the floor of the pit was a rough stone building, sometimes with several rooms. The body of the king or queen was placed inside the stone tomb, along with precious objects made of gold, silver, copper, carnelian and lapis lazuli. Very unusually, these burials also contained sacrificial victims,

killed to join their ruler. The bodies of these victims, along with vehicles and the animals that pulled them, were carefully laid out on the floor of the pit, dressed in very rich jewellery. Some were even provided with musical instruments. The pit was then filled with soil.

The Sumerians believed that when a person died they went to an underworld, which was thought to be a very quiet, shadowy place.

If a person was not given a proper burial they might, however, return as a ghost and cause illness. So it was important to offer the dead food and drink, which was brought to the grave on special days.

One Sumerian myth, or story involving the gods, tells how the goddess Inana journeyed to the underworld because she wanted to be queen there as well as in heaven. But nobody who entered the underworld could ever leave it – not even the gods. Inana was trapped. She managed to find a way to escape by choosing her husband, Dumuzi, to replace her in the underworld.

▲ **Jewellery from Royal Graves**

NEXT

Discover more Sumerian myths

The Sumerians told many stories about heroes and gods. Some of the most famous tales were composed by poets in the royal courts at cities such as Ur and Uruk. Here they celebrated earlier kings and told stories of their wisdom and courage.

Enmerkar and the lord of Aratta

Enmerkar, the king of Uruk, sends a messenger to the ruler of Aratta demanding that he send skilled workers to Uruk – together with the region's precious metals and stones – in order to build temples. The messenger travels over 'seven mountains' (which stands for a very long distance) to reach Aratta. However, when he delivers his message, the lord of Aratta refuses to agree. Instead the two kings challenge each other to a competition of riddles to see who is the cleverest. After several challenges back and forward, Enmerkar prepares to send a messenger again to demand that Aratta give up. As the message is too long for the messenger to learn it, Enmerkar writes it on a clay tablet – and so writing is invented. The lord of Aratta, unable to read the signs in the clay, realises that he has been defeated by a cleverer king.

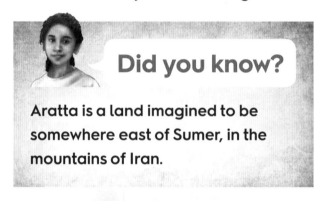

Did you know?

Aratta is a land imagined to be somewhere east of Sumer, in the mountains of Iran.

Bilgames and Huwawa

Wanting to be remembered as a hero, Bilgames, along with his servant Enkidu and 50 young men, sets out from Uruk to find the finest cedar trees to cut down. After crossing seven mountains (that is, travelling a very long way) the king discovers some magnificent trees and begins to chop at them with his axe. The guardian of the forest, the demon Huwawa, appears, surrounded by seven terrifying supernatural forces. Bilgames cleverly offers Huwawa gifts, in exchange for which the demon hands over his protective forces. When the seventh force has been given up, Bilgames leans towards Huwawa as if to give him a kiss of friendship – but instead he punches him on the face. The opportunity is taken to tie up Huwawa, but the demon is now in tears and Bilgames takes pity on him. However, his servant Enkidu then warns Bilgames that the only way that he will be remembered as a hero is through the death of Huwawa, so the demon is cruelly killed.

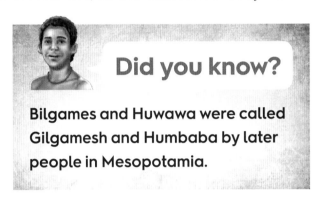

Did you know?

Bilgames and Huwawa were called Gilgamesh and Humbaba by later people in Mesopotamia.

Flood

The gods have created humans and animals. One day the ruler Ziusudra (whose name means 'life of distant days') hears a message from one of the gods telling him that a great flood will come. The gods have decided to destroy humanity because their noise is disturbing the sleep of the supreme god Enlil. A storm comes and rages for seven days and seven nights, while Ziusudra, along with people and animals, rides it out in a sealed boat. When the storm ends the king drills an opening in the boat and the sun enters. Once on dry land the animals disembark and Ziusudra makes an offering of oxen and sheep in gratitude. The god Enlil appears to him, having realised that the gods need humans as their servants. He rewards the king by giving him eternal life in the land of Dilmun, a place at the end of the earth where the sun rises.

Did you know?

The boat built by Ziusudra was shaped like a large round bowl, a type of vessel known as a coracle.

NEXT

Discover how Sumerian came to an end – except in Mesopotamian schools

From Sumer to Babylon to today

Across the world, over time, many languages have stopped being spoken because they have been replaced by others. For example, nobody today speaks ancient Egyptian, which has been replaced by Arabic. The same is true for the Sumerian language.

By around 2000 BC probably only a few people still spoke Sumerian. Most of the people in Mesopotamia used Akkadian. However, because Sumerian was understood as a language connected with religion and knowledge, the scribes continued to write it.

Trainee scribes in schools would learn to write Sumerian even though they spoke Akkadian. They would copy out texts in Sumerian and translate them into Akkadian, or the other way around.

Scribal schools were important for training officials when the city of Babylon became powerful; under King Hammurabi (1790–1750 BC), it conquered nearly all the other cities of Mesopotamia. Hammurabi wanted to show that he took justice for his people very seriously, as the earlier kings of Sumer had done, so he had some of his laws written down.

They were carved in cuneiform script (see page 15) onto a large standing stone (known as a stele). However, these laws were now written in the Akkadian language.

The young scribes studied not only ancient Sumerian but also mathematics. They continued to count in 10s and 60s, just as the first Sumerian scribes had done a thousand years before.

Today, counting in 60s is perhaps the most obvious thing that can be traced back to the Sumerians. For example, when we measure time we count 60 seconds in a minute and 60 minutes in an hour. The day is divided into 12 hours of the day and 12 hours of the night (12 is one-fifth of 60, that is 12 x 5 = 60). A circle is divided into 360 equal parts or degrees, which is a multiple of 60 (6 x 60 = 360).

◄ Stele of Hammurabi

Did you know?

Although it was mainly boys who learnt to be scribes, occasionally girls would also be taught to read and write.

CONGRATULATIONS

Name..

You have discovered ancient Sumer.
You can be described in Sumerian as SHU-DU-A,
which means perfect or well done.

First published in the United kingdom by the Ashmolean Museum, Publications Department, Beaumont Street, Oxford OX1 2PH

ISBN 978-1-910807-36-1

British Library Cataloguing in Publication Data

A catalogue record for this book is available from the British Library

Designed by Mark Tilley-Watts

Illustrated by Niall Harding/D'Avila Illustration Agency

Printed and bound in the UK by Gomer Press

All images are copyright of the Ashmolean Museum, with the exception of: (p.1) compass iStockphoto; (p.9) locust iStockphoto; (p.11) clay cone mosaic WikiCommons; (p.12) sickle Alamy; (p. 17) lapis lazuli iStockphoto; (p. 26) sheep iStockphoto

For further details about the Ashmolean Museum's publications please visit: www.ashmolean.org/shop

ASHMOLEAN
MUSEUM
OXFORD